The

FUTURE MIRACLE

of

YESTERDAY

CEDRIC LOGAN

Published in the United States of America

Brilliant Books Literary
137 Forest Park Lane Thomasville
North Carolina 27360 USA

ISBN:
Paperback: 979-8-88945-305-5
Ebook: 979-8-88945-306-2

WHERE TO BEGIN

I didn't know how I was going to start this. I didn't even know if I would ever finish this book. But I told myself this is something I had to do. I owed it to myself to do this. I hope if you are reading this that this can help change your life in some way for the better. Well in order for me to start this off right I should tell you who I used to be. That was alter ego. He was a representative. A person I wanted everyone to see. I once was that guy. His name was Xavier. We will call him "X" for short. The one thing I have always admired about him was his fearlessness. I mean this guy would look danger right in the face and have nerves of steel with a determination and almost rebellious defiance as if to say that the opposition was not going to break him, defeat him or deter him. I looked up to that guy and honestly I felt I grew a lot into who I was supposed to be all these years but just never discovered it because of his experiences. We never had a conversation, but I knew that he respected me. Kind of like one of those unspoken guy code type things. But it was mutual. It was mutual. He was the person I saw when I looked in the mirror. He was my alter ego. But he was not who I was but he was the person everyone saw. It wasn't until I found out who I truly was that I actually start to live. It all started with a moment of reflection.

As I look back over my life, and I reminisce over all my experiences, I am reminded of what my grandmother told me a few years back. She said "Cedric you have a story to tell and if you keep on living your story will write itself". When I first heard her say that I didn't pay too much attention to it because how can someone like me have anything to give to the world. I brushed it off not knowing how prophetic her word would be in my life. I wish I knew then what I know now. Now in the 29 years of being alive, I have encountered some life's most devastating struggles and greatest triumphs and victories. And throughout every journey and each stage of my life that I have overcome this far. Look the truth of the matter is I am turning 30 next year and I have been a lot of places and done a lot of thins but yet still I haven't hit the pinnacle I have wanted to reach. I'm not gonna lie I have had a lot of ups and downs in theses few decades. I have achieved greatness on the proverbial "Top of the Mountain". I have seen some of the most beautiful sights that the world has to offer. O yes I have seen Mother Earth's beauty and the tranquility it brings. I have also seen the wrath and vengeance of Father Time's anger. I been to war I have seen death hit several people closest to me. I know the bitterness and heartbreak from a bad divorce and several relationships after that. The pain and traumatic events that I have witness has really took a toll on a lot of areas of my life. But no matter what the one thing that stayed with me is that who you have in your life will determine where your life will become if you don't have your identity. You know the whole "Birds of a Feather" "Guilt by Association" type deal.

But yea back to about why I am writing this, well that answer is very simple. I recently had a daughter and she is a miracle … literally. She has really changed my life for the better. That's why I name her Miracle Elizabeth Logan because she is such a… uh you get the point. But anyways I am writing her some words of wisdom that I have learned from my experiences that she can read and apply when she is older because she is just a baby right now. Let me tell you for 10 month old she is so smart. I love her so much.

What am I going say to my daughter in here that I want her to have for a lifetime. I really wish she could understand me right now. This whole book is basically my time capsule of truth and knowledge that I have acquired through all my trial and errors that I want to share with her so she always have something that she can take with her for a lifetime. What nuggets of wisdom would I give her you ask? Well when she reads this I want her to first off how much her father loves her very much. I hope when she get older I hope she enjoyed reading this as much as I did writing this. But I hope that that if you are reading this and going through some things in your life that my words can motivate you to strive for the greatness that is inside of you to overcome it.

So here the deal baby girl. Now that the readers have been briefed as to what to expect from this I need to have a daddy daughter talk with you. I have watch you grow from a beautiful baby girl to the young adult that are becoming today. I am so proud of you and all the great things that you have done and all the awesome things you are going to do. You are getting ready to start your new life and new adventures and I know you might be nervous. But fear not my little Miracle Whip (Yes I still call you that) your father wants to share some things that he has learned over the years and I believe that it will help as you transition into the real world. I have faith that you apply these principles that I am going to teach you and you be the best miracle you can be. I'm not going to overwhelm you with hundreds upon hundreds pages of things to read. This is not a novel. I am going to keep it short, sweet and to the point. Just a few chapters. You can handle that right? You loved reading with me when you're just a little girl... This will be no different. I just know you will benefit from this I have already cried the tears of joy when you were born, and will be there to wipe the tears from yours if you take heed from your good old dad. Alright here is the moment of truth and the million dollar question: Are you going to turn the page or put the book down and say this isn't for me? Dun Dun Dun. Just playing. I already know the answer to that so I will see you there.

THESE ARE THE FACTS

See. I know I raised my daughter right. Ha Ha. Miracle I am so glad you chose to turn that page. I love how your curiosity drove you to turn the page to learn something new. That's a great quality to have baby girl. Never stop learning it is the essence of our survival.

Well, hey let's just get right to then shall we. Miracle as you get older and life begins to remove the innocence of your youth, you will find, (which by now sure you are already experiencing it) that life is tough. Really tough. It can be a very mean and scary place.

But when you have faith in God and a resilient mindset there isn't anything that you can overcome. I still remember all the memories we have made over the years. In that time though you have taught me so much in your young age. I guess that was just as scary to be a first time daughter as it was me being a first time dad. But hey we made it through didn't we. Exactly!! I am going to share with you what you have taught me over the years since you are older and I know you can appreciate the nuggets of wisdom I will give and apply them to your everyday life. But hear me Miracle when I say this: I do NOT have all the answers. Anybody that says they have all the answers don't trust them at all. I am not perfect by any means we are all human. I have made a lot of mistakes in my life. I have made bad choices. I have failed. But I want you to know that I did the best I could to be a good provider and the best father I can be to you princess. I say this because I want you to be better than me. In fact I want you to be the best version of you, you can be. I don't want you to fall into the same holes that I did and have to experience pain like I had to. Your mother and I named you miracle for a reason. I want you to excel in ways unimaginable and reach your ultimate potential. I know that might seem like I'm putting a lot of pressure on you and just being mean ole dad right now, but I need you to understand that all I want is the best for you and I need you to be prepared for the real world. You know outside of the cell phones social media and latest dance trend. It is my duty to make sure you have all the tools you need to survive and not only that but to thrive. I cannot take this duty light and I can't afford to fail you and have you unprepared. I promise in this book you will read things in here that have been used repeatedly. This is intentional. I want you to pay extra attention to this. I love you and I always will.

YOU ARE WHAT
YOU DRINK.

No Miracle. You did not read that wrong. I know that you are used to the expression "you are what you eat" which is true in its own right, however, what you drink on a daily basis can tell you a lot about your life in ways you never thought about. You get it. No. ok remember when you were younger and I would always get you to drink water and you would always want soda. I remember you came to me one day asking for something to drink and I told you to drink some water. You said you did not want water you wanted some soda. She left and came back and asked again I told you that you couldn't have a soda right now because you were getting one for dinner.

Whoopee did you throw a temper tantrum you did not want high quality H2O. I mean it was the good spring water that you have to drive to Kroger's and pay 3 bucks for the case too. After about 30 minutes of having an attitude of not having a soda you finally calmed down and came to me again and asked for something to drink. Again I told you again to drink some water. But then something Miraculous happened. You not going to believe this. You drunk some water and it actually quenched your thirst. I can honestly say that you had a ball the rest of your day and you was in a better mood than when you first asked me for something to drink. This is just like life. Think about that soda you wanted so bad. Now imagine that I shook the can up hard before I gave it to you what do you think would happened? Exactly. Soda would explode out the can and spill on the floor leaving less soda for you to enjoy Life and people are going to shake you up in the real world baby girl. The stuff that's on the inside of you: your beliefs, your values, your identity will determine what you let come out. Now I want you to remember how good that water tasted the first time you took that first sip after having an attitude. Now imagine if I would have shook that bottle up before I gave it to you. You know what would happen? Absolutely nothing. You would have a full bottle of water to enjoy. I have always taught you bible verses and one of my favorite verses is "Out of the abundance of the heart the mouth speaketh" which means what you harbor inside of you will become your identity. It consumes you. It engulfs. It literally becomes who you are. This mean if we are bitter or have hate or despair in our hearts because of the past that will be what comes out of you. You are very fragile and you must be like that water and keep faith and love in your heart and know that even though that even though the world we living in isn't perfect the fact that you are in it makes it one step closer. So miracle after hearing this I got a question for you? Are you thirsty?

DON'T GO BLIND TRYING TO FOCUS

I wonder if you are reading this and thinking that this statement doesn't make any sense right. I must mean if I focus directly into the sun then I'll go blind that's common sense dad. I hope not because that would be proving my point. You are focusing on the statement itself instead the message that it has. Let me explain it this way. Do you remember the time I took you to our family reunion for memorials day and we had to take that 3 hour flight. When left the airport to get on the plane you were looking out the window and you were in awe of how big the planes.

I mean you stared in amazing. So much so that you didn't even pay attention to the fact that I was trying to give you a snack. More for me then. Ha Ha. But I remember that when the plane took off and we started to ascend into to sky the once gigantic plane took its hold off your attention span and you begin to beg for your snack that I was this close to eating. Miracle when you focus on something everything else around seems to disappear so if you are focusing the drama and problems and failures you will be blind to the blessings around you. Once you focus all your energy in to being a better you and learning all you can all of you problems that you once found so big that you thought that you would overcome or survived. But you are a witness baby girl you focused on bettering yourself and you eventually you made your weakness your strengths. I am so proud that you learning this quality at such a young age, but now I need you to magnify this trait because the real world is not something you must not take lightly. But just know that even though life has its ugly moments, it will always as beautiful as you allow it to be. Don't look at your problems like they are gigantic. Do not let it overwhelm you. Face it head on. I know it might seem scary at first. But be brave. It is ironic that in the bible we find that the phase "Do not be afraid" was written 365 times. Think of it as a wakeup call for every day of the year. Live everyday fearlessly.

LIFE CAN BE A BEACH IF YOU DON'T FILL YOUR BUCKET UP WITH JUST SAND

Even though you were born in the cold winter month of December, you really loved the summer months. I mean you could not wait for summer to get here so you can go splash at the pool. Hey do you remember that summer you were with me and I took you to the beach. You were so happy and excited. For some reason, you really liked the sand and I guess how it felt grinding it between your fingers. You had a little red bucket and a whole bunch of small toys (of which I think you way too many toys that day) and a shovel. So when we found a good place to set up our stuff, you sat down, emptied your bucket and started playing. As you were playing, I noticed that you would fill the bucket almost to the brim. I thought you were trying to make a sand castle at first but you would just kick the bucket over. You did this a couple of time until one time you just filled it up to the brim and then just stopped. You looked up and saw a big wave coming and wanted to get closer to it and pick up some rocks. I remember telling you to pick all your toys up so we can move closer. I watched you as I was getting the lawn chairs, try to put all the toys you brought into a bucket completely filled with sand. You were starting to get frustrated after several failed attempt. So I told you to just dump the bucket so you can put your toys and moved. You reluctantly dumped the bucket and we got closer. You seemed a little quiet and distant as you were playing and picking up rocks to add to her collections in her bucket. As it was getting closer to time to leave, I told you to pack up your stuff so we can head out. You looked sad as you packed all the toys and rocks you had collected to the brim. You told me that wish you could have took some sand home but you didn't think that there was any space left. Do you remember what I told you? I told you that sand is very small it will make a way in there. I watched you face light up as you saw me grab a handful of sand and shake it around in the bucket like a gourmet chef seasoning meat just to make you laugh even harder. In that moment I realized that Miracle you are just like that bucket. You want to be able to get everything in your bucket. I'm not gonna lie I really did not want you to bring all them toys but as I got older I realized that you needed those toys. These toys represent your family and faith and experience. You wanted them there because they were your friends and you felt safe with them because they always had your back. You really picked out some pretty great rocks that day. In life these stones are you're your careers your friends your education. These are always changing. You are going to lose some stones every now and then. But that's ok. Life has plenty pebbles for you to acquire as you to continue to get older. Now the sand is tricky but in hind sight it is actually very simplistic. The sand is literally everything else. The stress and hardships of life. Every circumstance, every problem, every situation that life has put you in. It is in those hard and trying moments that we allow our little everyday problems fill our lives up with frustration, depression, drama, hopelessness, and bitterness just like that sand did your bucket baby girl. I know. I have been there. Miracle, when your life is filled with disorder and chaos, you have no space for the family, friends and important people who is supposed to be in your life to help you progress. It prevents us from having family bonds and things that are most important in life. You start isolating yourself. Trust me when I tell you from experience. You don't want to be on the preverbal island like that. It gets very lonely. I mean yea I would like to go back to that island but I don't want end up like "Gilligan". But that's beside the point. All I am saying is if what you are going through right now. Now I want you to ask yourself "Will this affect me 5 years from now". If the answer is no don't waste 5 more minutes worrying about it my child. Now before I go any further there is almost something I forgot to mention which is maybe the most important tool you have. Prayer. You must always pray and tap into that higher source that gives you the strength and abilities to achieve and endure life's obstacles. Because how you can let your light shine if you do not have any power. We are all here for a divine purpose. Something bigger than ourselves. It is up to us to stay plugged up the source of energy and power by staying in constant prayer. It doesn't have to be one of the long deacon prayers of the church that you hear every Sunday at church. You can keep it short if you want. It's all going to the same place. Continue to tap into you power. Manifest your destiny. Life awaits you!! The only person that can put a limitation on how great you can be is you. Always remember that. You are enough. I also want you to come up with an ex-bucket list. Make a list everything you are never going to do again. Remember all those places you used to go. Those things that you used to do that got you in trouble, caused you pain or set you back. You don't have to cross anything out and it will be your daily reminder on how to progress and evolve into your greatness.

IT'S LONELY AT THE BOTTOM BUT IT'S CROWDED AT THE TOP

I know that you have heard different. From the songs, movies etc. but if you really think about it, isn't that like the furthest thing from the truth. It seems like when you first starting your business nobody wants to support you. Because let's face it they do not know you. Or, what is worse you will have people you do know that won't support you. It's lonely when you are first starting out but this is the best time to see who to take with you when you elevate to the prosperous season of your life. Because you will notice that once a person gets recognized in high regards or becomes a celebrity as they call them, everybody I mean everybody comes out of the woodworks try to jump on their bandwagon. I hope one day you will have a vision of what you are destined to do. You will one day have a dream that you will desperately want. I did. I always dreamt that one day I'd be a famous actor. When I first started my pursuit of this dream and was going to the networking events, and trying to make a name for yourself, telling your people to support you, I didn't have that many people supporting you outside of your family. As a matter of fact they were shooting down my ideas not knowing the success it possess. But hey I worked with the little I had. Those were hard times. We really were at rock bottom and little to no one was there. But notice how, as you begin to get a little attention and your social media following increases that suddenly your social status does to. Then when you reach a certain "social status" you have those same people that turned you down and doubted will be right there to try to see if they can find a way to benefits off you. Now, I am no celebrity but I do know that sadly in today's society money and fame determines success. Always be humble. Always be hungry. Because when you humble you remember those that were with you in the trenches and will still go to war for you and it makes you generous because you want to give back. When you are hungry you stay motivated. You stay ready so you don't have to get ready. You always preparing for your legacy. I know you have it in you. Be loyal to those that are loyalty. Be compassionate and forgiving of others but don't be naïve and let people take advantage of you. But most importantly, give somebody a shot when you become successful. Never forgot that someone had to give you opportunities to achieve all that you will achieve. The last thing that I want you to get out of this chapter is work in silence. Don't tell everyone one your next move. I had an old army buddy tell me something when we were in Iraq and it stuck with me to this day. They told me that people will support you when you doing well just never better than them. Everybody is not on your team baby girl. As a matter of fact the reality is that are people in your life that are in your corner as you are convenient to them or have something that they need. I tell you all the time. You were here for a purpose. But when you can no longer serve their purpose and benefit them they will abandon you when you need them the most. But don't let this stop you or deter you from attaining greatness. Don't waste time trying to make time for people not worth your time. Because the good news is as you get older and life gives you more experience you will be able to sort those people out and remove them from your life and have true people remain. You will almost never lose our family and friends but over time if you focused you will realize who your real friends are. Surround yourself with the people that are on the same mission that you are on. You will never lose Miracle when you try anything. Because you will achieve your objection or you will learn a valuable lesson. Continue to invest in yourself and promote your legacy until you see the fruits of your labor. People will do one of two things. They will get mad and not support you or they will get inspired and support your cause. Just know your dad is always in your corner I'm so proud of you.

TURN THOSE
SCARS INTO YOUR
BEAUTY MARKS

Alright you made it to this point. It's kind of ironic that when writing this chapter I got a paper cut. I have always been astonished by what value the skin adds to the human body though. When you were 10 months old I remember I was holding you in my arms. I remember you put your tiny little hands in mine. I had a scar on my wrist that I was hiding from you from when I burned myself on the stove (I know you get freaked out at the sign of cut burns and bruises). But you kept pulling my hand to see what it what is

I was hiding because you thought I had some candy that I was keeping from you. But when you saw the scar on my hand you started laughing. I mean you had your little tongue out just laughing. Then out of nowhere you started reaching for my face as if you were trying to give me hug and make me feel better. That melted my heart that day. What I'm saying here is that some time we are going to make mistakes. We don't always make the right choice and decision. These action have consequences as I'm sure you know that by now by the times you were on punishment at my house. But in life can get a little deeper and painful than just a spanking or getting your toys and cell phone taken away from you. In life certain mistakes can result in failed relationships, injuries, prison sentences and even fatal consequences. I am not saying this to scare you. I just need you to understand that what everything that has been happening in the world with societies view on what is deemed acceptable you cannot forget the teachings you had received from your family and your experiences. But even when you do mess up and go through those pains and sorrows, (Which we all do.) understand that nobody is perfect. You must forgive yourself first and foremost. You have a purpose. You are here for a reason. The experiences that you have faced and will endure are meant to be a lesson to teach you how to make you stronger and prepare you for the next phases of your life. Take it from me. I learned the hard way. You have 100% of your worst days and I bet that never occurred to you. The pain you felt 5 years ago. 10 years. Yeah it may still hurt even to this day but it doesn't sting as much now. Does it? These scars are your testimony to the world that you overcame what you went through. Just like when we used crawl around roaring like tigers when you were younger. You are a tiger be proud of those scars. They are representation of your stripes. Miracle I promise you the day that you learn to forgive yourself and others and keep that "scars and stripes" mentality I promise your enemies will soon wave their white flags. Because when it is all said and done and you look in the

THE FUTURE MIRACLE OF YESTERDAY

mirror all those scar hurts trail and errors, you really made it through and overcame something you thought was impossible. So straighten up your crown my little princess as walked into your future like a boss. You have a whole kingdom waiting for you.

BE A SPONGE NOT A DOPPELGANGER

E verybody has a "Hero". Whether they want to admit it or not. Everybody has that person or people that want to be just like and often find ways to imitate them in your everyday life. Whether it is a celebrity on television or a minister at a church everywhere you turn around someone is looking up to someone else. I would like to believe that I was somewhat of a hero to you growing up and even to this day. But I will still love you even if I'm not lol. But anyways on Saturdays you would wake me up at 8 AM in the morning just so you can have your cereal and watch some SpongeBob Square pants. You love that show so much because like watching SpongeBob inhale and suck up everything. When I saw that it immediately remind me of you. I mean besides you eating up everything in sight, but that fact that you were absorbing everything that I was doing. You were learning everything so quickly it amazed me and made so proud to be a father. Oh but I remember a certain little princess that got mad when somebody change the channel to Justice League. You didn't like how superman was fighting his "evil twin brother". It all makes sense now. See what I'm telling you that you need to absorb the right information from the right people who want you to succeed. Wisdom is all around you. But it up to you to go get it the one thing I want you to take from this chapter is that there is only 1 Miracle Elizabeth Logan and I don't ever need you to feel like you need to grind and give your blood sweat and tears into something only for people to compare you to someone else. Be the best Miracle you can be. I know you can do it. You have what it takes. Don't let anybody tell you different. You were born uniquely different than everybody else in the entire world and you don't have to try to be anyone else. The world needs the real you. Not a carbon copy. Not a factory prototype. The authentic evolution of you the women you are destined to be. The gifts that you possess can impact the world in a way that can make it a better place. But YOU have to do it princess. You have such a free spirit. Let it continue to fly. Let people admire it from afar or with you. But never let any cage your spirit. Never lose yourself to anyone but God. Never give away your story. It's yours to tell and I know it will be a best-seller. Be your own boss because if you are not going to be a boss, you are going to work for one. Embrace your authentic potential. You are a Leader and leaders build ladders of success instead of climbing them princess.

PREPARE YOURSELF FOR THE MARRIAGE NOT THE WEDDING

N ow I'm going to real transparent with you right now. This chapter was very difficult and emotional for me to write. I literally wrote this in a Chick–Fil-A booth at 8:45 AM on a Friday morning waiting for a client to arrive for a business meeting. The reason it is so hard is because I know we have never really sat down and really talked about me and your mother divorcing, I'm sure you have a lot of question. But I need you to understand that regardless of what happened between me and you mother that we both love you very much and that will never change. I know you have a lot of mixed emotion and it makes you sad at times. I am sure if you are reading this then you are old enough to understand that me and your mother were not happy and we just eventually grew apart. I know you don't want to hear this but in hind sight we are both better people when we are apart. It made it easier to raise you into the amazing woman you are becoming. You probably think that I am the last person you would qualify to talk to you about this, you might be right. As I have stated I'm not perfect but as a father the last thing I would ever want if for you to get your heartbroken princess. That is every father's worst nightmare. You are so special and fragile so whenever you are sad and I see you cry I instantly go into super daddy mode only because my heart cannot bear it. So before you completely ignore this chapter at least hear me out. Listen miracle as much as I hate to admit because I am overprotective of you I don't know how I am going to feel when it's time to give you away at your wedding. Even now as I am writing this, I am looking at you sleep peacefully in your crib. I mean you are so tiny, and now I am supposed to just give you away to another man to take over all the duties and responsibility that I have done your whole life. It's a very hard bitter sweet pill to swallow. Now I gotta level with you because it seems like these days everybody puts more effort and preparation into the wedding than what the wedding actually symbolizes, marriage, the lifelong commitment that it is. Now, I have to say this because I don't want to seem biased. "Some people are not ready for marriage" so my words of wisdom for this chapter is before you walk that aisle make sure you know the person you are marrying. Believe me miracle it is harder than it looks if you do not know what you are doing. The only way you will know your mate is to ask questions. Get to know everything you can. Understand a person will always be who they are. It's just that when you first meet someone you like who put your best foot forward because you want to make a good impression. So you kinda hide your flaws that you think might cause a rejection until you have been together long enough to feel comfortable to show them. That is why you hear people that are having problems in their relationship say things like "he or she changed" and " they are not the same person that I once knew" when the truth they in fact the same person you are just realizing who they really were. People do not change over time, but if they really love you they will evolve for the better for you. This why it is important that you ask questions, and not only ask questions but ask the right questions. It's cool to know what their favorite colors and their hobbies but what about what the goals are for the future, his relationship with his mom. This is a big one because how a man treats his mother is a direct reflection of how he will treat you. Never feel bad about asking questions and learning all you can about anyone that is wanting to come into your space. Remember that the person you are going to marry is someone you are going to invest your time, energy and your essence with. In the earlier chapters I told you about how the people you allow in your circle can have a big role how your life can be impacted. Ask yourself right now: "Would I marry myself right now?" Do you believe the answer is yes? Would you be able to live with yourself and put up with the things you do? Take it from me. It's easy to get to the wedding. But making a marriage work is probably one of the hardest things to do. But miracle always remember, Marriage is difficult. I want you to treat you marriage like you are a CEO of a Fortune 500 company. Remember the first time you filled out an online application for that job. Didn't you hate the fact that when you uploaded your resume when you went to the next screen it would ask you to manually fill out you employment history. It is so irritating that you would have answer question and re-answer the same questions. Be just like that. These owners thoroughly go through all these applications to find the right candidate to fill that position. They understand that who they hire will have a major role in the outcome of the success of the company. They are not just going to hire anybody. I have already expressed to you in the earlier chapters of the importance of who you allow in your space. Who you decide to marry is that much more serious. It's ok to pray that you one day get a husband. It is every girls dream at one point in time or another. However if you want to have the best But it is not impossible, and when the time comes that a young man finally sweeps you off your feet and you two jump the broom, just know I will be so proud to give you away but you will always be daddy's little princess.

KNOW YOUR WORTH

T his chapter ties into a lot of the other chapters. But it is uniquely different. It has the same message, but it comes from the inward perceptions that you possess. This chapter is all about how YOU see yourself and a different way to understand your value. The best way I get you to understand this is to use the example you have always seemed to be able to understand... Money!!! In the previous chapter I gave you tips of what to look for in a mate and how to prepare for your marriage. But I didn't tell you how to where to start. I did that for a reason. Just to show that sometime when do not know who we are as an individual we go looking for things we are not ready or prepared to accept. It's easy to say send me this relationship or send me this job, or send me this opportunity. But don't you know if you not preparing yourself grooming yourself for what you are asking for then when you finally get what you have been asking for you be able to appreciate it. I want you think of this scenario in many perspective. Imagine that a guy finds 50 dollars in his jacket. He goes outside and sees 1 dollar on the floor. He goes to pick up the dollar but when he does the 50 dollar bill falls out of his back pocket. Do you think he will happy to the fact that was a dollar richer, or will he be upset that he lost 50 dollars trying to get it? The first way I want you to look at this is that when it is your turn you will be blessed big time. When this happens do not get the proverbial big head. This sense of entitlement that world owes you anything. They say that "The grass is always greenest where you water it" Don't worry about trying to get what someone already has because if roll the dice chances are you will lose what you possess trying to take another. You must always stay humble because with humility comes hope. Hope is the first step in happiness which if you live long enough, will give you your heavenly purpose.

I also want you to look at that 50 dollar bill. I want you be like that in the jacket of life. I want you conduct yourself in a manner so great that you will always be "The one that got away" and not "A dodged bullet". You carry the legacy of our name when you walk out that door. You must know who you are and stand firm on your beliefs. The world has yet to see the greatness that you have inside. Unleash it.

You know it funny. When I held you for the first time when you were a baby, I knew you were priceless. I knew that there was no amount of money that could pay for the love that I had for you. I knew that you were going to be something great in this world. I know that you

MASK ON. MASK OFF

I t is only fitting that this chapter have this name because I know you love this song and you are the future I even wrote a song to this song for you when you were 6 months old that I played for you on your 1st birthday and every birthday since. But I want to you look at this from a different point of view. When I was younger I used to look at animals in the wild on TV, and there was a scene where a tiger was trying to eat an eagle of all things. He climbed this tree and literally jumped out of the tree trying to catch his sitting prey out of the air. But he was too far from the eagle and nearly died after falling nearly 30 feet to the ground below. Thinking back a lot of people in the world are just like that tiger. The first thing I want to you to learn from this tiger is that best response to antagonist is to not to fight. Sometimes in times their will be people that come into your life simply to use you and build them self-up. These people will do everything they can just to bring you down and act outside of your character. DO NOT GIVE THEM THE SATISFACTION! You have to you use your head and play it smart. They say that information is better than ammunition. Sometimes you have to act like you don't know anything and get all the info you can on the situation. People will always be on the best behavior when they know they are being watched, but when you have nothing to offer to someone and that person can't benefit from you, their true character will be revealed. Something else I want you take away from this is that there will be people and things that come in your life disguised as a great opportunity. Be careful with these, these more than likely are traps that can have worse off than when you first started they come in the form of an old flame, a job The tiger saw the eagle as an opportunity to feed his belly but not only did he not get fed he almost died and was buzzard food itself. There will be times and situations in which you are so confused and don't know how to handle it. But when you don't know what to do when you are in those situations, I want you to pray and be patient and have faith and the answers will come to you my child

IT'S GOOD TO HAVE JUICE, BUT YOU REALLY WANT THAT SAUCE

One of the best memories of you is when you were 10 maybe 11 months old. You loved to eat. A lot. I mean as soon as you seen or smelled food you would immediately to get to it. Whether it was me or your grandparent wherever the food was there you were. You were crawling a lot more and you would crawl to me and always want me to pick you up and give you some of my food. Well on that particular day I was getting your lunch together. Cinnamon Applesauce. Your favorite back then. Mainly because your teeth did not want to come in just yet. But anyways

CEDRIC LOGAN

I remember you were playing on your mat with your toys and you were sipping some juice out of your sippy cups. I grabbed the big jar of applesauce out of the refrigerator and as soon as you saw that jar you looked at your sippy cup with the juice and threw it across the room. I never seen a baby crawl that fast. But thinking back you made me so proud and you taught me a valuable lesson that day. That juice you drinking in your cup didn't seem to last. Kind of like the thing we show to the world for attention and praise. We flash our cars, clothes and other materialistic things and are only here for a season. These are temporary and they will eventually be of no use to us. But that applesauce lasted that whole week and you loved every bite of it. See when you have the sauce it is something that last a lifetime. These are skills you pick up. Crafts that you work on. This is the knowledge that you learned along the way. If someone gets into an accident and they total their car,they will never be able to use that car again. But if that person learns how to build cars then they will always have transportation. I want you to leave a legacy on this earth that is all your own. I want to be like that fisherman that will not only give you some of the fish I have, but teach you how to fish so you will be able to eat for a Lifetime. Learn all you can. Read all you can. Do not stop learning. I cannot stress this enough to you baby girl. Because when you look back on your life I do not want you to have any regrets. I want you to live. Truly live. Show the world what you are made of Miracle. Do it for you. Make yourself happy. Don't ever feel like you need to be perfect and go above and beyond to make me proud. I am proud of whatever gift or talents you possess, as long as you are giving your very best. That is all I ever want from you.

LEARN WHEN
TO LET GO

You know one of the celebrities I have yet to meet, and would like to would be none other than Dwayne "The Rock" Johnson. I remember something he said awhile back strolling on Instagram. I think he was in Vancouver. I believe he said "Sometimes the very thing want will be the best thing you never had". It just made me start to think. How many time do we fight so hard for things that are only good at the moment? I can remember plenty of times. I can remember the feeling of frustration, anger and resentment because I wasn't able to reach the goals that I was setting. But looking at where I am at now in my life I wouldn't have achieved half the things I have achieved. Everything happens for a reason. Don't be sad if you didn't get that job, or that opportunity didn't go through. Even if you lost that relationship. These are painful but these may have hurt a lot more if you dragged that pain out for 20 or 30 years. Your purpose is greater than your situations. What you have in store for your life can activated by you. Value yourself. I'm sure you have already figured this out by now. Life is not a free trial in a magazine. You don't get to cancel your subscription when life gets too hard. But luckily, you have a manager up above that you can always talk to. This chapter is also difficult for me because I always am so firm on you about never giving up. I hope you understand that I believe in that full heart-edly. However, sometime for the sake of your sanity and not losing who you are sometimes you just have to let go. I'm not going to lie to you baby girl. The world doesn't always have happy endings. There are heartbreaks and disappointment. The good guy doesn't always win and some relationships just do not last. No matter hard you want them to. That is why I told you in the earlier chapters about learning everything that you can about the person you are investing you essence with. You need to be aware of the fact that some people come into your life for the wrong reasons. If you are not careful you will become attached to. These people will control and manipulate your thoughts and emotions if you allow them to, some people are just there because you are convenient at the time. You have to pay attention to the signs because if you are not care-ful, will rob you of your youth and identity. I know it will be hard to cut these people because you have invested so much time into this person. You may even love them. I'll give you the benefit of the doubt. But nobody is worth your peace. Your mindset and outlook on life can be determined by who you are around. Remember, the ocean couldn't sink the Titanic until it was struck by an iceberg and water got into the ship. It will hurt to let these people go but the more you hold on the more painful it gets. When you finally just let go the pain slowly but surely start to evaporate. But in all that pain I want find some peace in the fact the all the negative people you have cut out of your life will be left with a version of you that simply will not exist anymore. They will always have a memory and have this image of you. But you should be excited about this because you have grown and evolved so much and that version of you that they have is not who you are anymore. They will never get the opportunity to experience who you have become in their absence. Now you got to remember that sometime those people will try to find a way to find a way back into you circle. People that did you wrong, hurt you, and try to break you down. Here is where things get tricky. Because you learned in the previous chapters that you have to forgive people. But Miracle I am a firm believer that just because you forgive a person you can love a person from a distance. You don't want to ever put yourself back into any situation that almost destroyed you. You have to understand that some people that no matter how they try some people are just not meant to be together. To help you understand I want you to think about playing tug of war with a car by yourself. We both know that you are not going to pull a car and you notice that the stronger you pull the rope your hand will be in even more pain. Now after all that pain of trying to pull it, what happens when you finally let go. How much better does your hand feel? This is just like life. The more we try to hang on the past and what could have been or would have been the more that life seems to hurt. The more that the pain consumes us. But when we learn to finally let all of the bitterness and regrets and finally forgive yourself just watch how easier you will be able to live life to your full potential. Never let and old flame burn you twice. Either burn the bridges that continually cause you pain or weigh you down or learn how to swim because there are no life vest in life and you will drown.

WHAT ARE
YOUR GOALS

This is one of the most important lessons I have to give to you Miracle. It is probably the most important things that I can teach outside of your faith in God. These are the goals that you have for your life. Now I'm sure your goals as a child are running wild right now. I am not going to shut down your dream or our life goals. But I just want you to put your goals and dreams into a different point of view. For starters instead of setting a goal focusing on just becoming a millionaire, try to focus on something that will make a positive impact on the world and leave a legacy. Because at the end of the day life is not about how many luxurious items you possess for finding the perfect mate it is about finding inner peace so you can make beautiful memories. The first thing you have to remember is that dreams without any action are simply glorified dreams. You can want to be successful. You can want that house, that relationship, and that job. But if you are not willing to work for what you want, and make the sacrifices and keep pushing forward even though everything and everyone are telling you to quit, then you will be like a hamster on a wheel, you will feel like you are making progress but you won't be going anywhere. One of my favorite actors is Will Smith. His role that he played in "The Pursuit of Happyness" resonated with me so much because when you were a baby I felt like I was literally living his life in the movie. I remember an interview when they asked how he became so successful. He said and I quote "I am not afraid to die on a treadmill" As he explained it became clear what he meant. He said that if you and him were both on a treadmill he was either going to die on that treadmill or you were going to get off the treadmill first. That stuck with me even to this day. This means that if you want to be successful you have to be willing to work harder and longer than everybody else. Don't be outworked. Don't be outdone. You have to be the first person starting and the last person leaving. There will be long nights. I can guarantee you that you will have setbacks and disappointments. But when you finally achieve your goals imagine how much more you are going to appreciate them because you will remember everything you had to do to achieve them. But remember before anything else, that in order to make your dreams come true you have to first …. WAKEUP!!!

GRAND FINALE

W e have finally made to the end. I am so proud that you read it to the end. I know parts may have been confusion right now because you are so young but like the elders say "just keep on living" and you will see how everything I have shown you in this book will all come together and make sense. Miracle I just want you to know that you were born into chaos. I know there are times you felt alone but I need to you to know that your dad has always been there for you whether you realize it or not. I want you to change the world. I want you to impact the community in such a way that other lives can change. Just know that whatever you do with your life it is your path to choose. I will guide you as much as I can to make sure you have every opportunity that I never had to excel and thrive and become the best version you that you can be. We have our own story to tell so keep living and your story will write itself. Now I thought about how to close the chapters on this book. I came to the conclusion that the best way to end it is to bring the material that I was going to use originally for this book... My poems. Believe it or not this was just going to be a book of poems. But I have so much that want to teach you and I wanted make this first book special. So in closing here is some of my work and I hope it inspires you to write your own life's story

POEMS

WHO'S THAT IN THE MIRROR

When you look into the mirror
What is it that you see
Do you see the person you want
Or someone everybody wants you too be

When you look at your reflection
Do you passion in their eyes
That everlasting spirit
Of a fire that refuses to die

Or is it a stranger with a mask
Hiding pain and shame you won't show
Haunted by your sins of the past
That just won't allow you to grow

If you could conversate with that person
How would that dialogue read
Would you tell them what they want to hear
Or the reality of what they really need

And what would their response be
If the alternate universe was true
I wonder what your reflection would think
And what would be their impression of you

THE FUTURE MIRACLE OF YESTERDAY

Do you think they would be happy
Of the life choices you create
Or would they want to switch places
To prevent you from future mistakes

Do you say to this person in the mirror
You can't be a friends
Sad that one of you greatest allies
You treat like a WORST enemy

No see the person that wanna be
And who you currently are
Is a constant battle with your spirit and your flesh
Who will always be at war

If all you can see is bad
Where your essence is fully grown
If focus creates blindness
What are you really focusing on

As you take the time to pause
Your priorities become clearer
You can choose to see destiny or despair
When you look into the mirror

So again

If you looked at your reflection
What would you see
I hope to choose to your greatness
So you walk in your destiny.

Manifest your destiny
Everyone has a opinion
Of what makes a man a man
What qualifies them for that title

CEDRIC LOGAN

Well let me help you if I can
Now I don't have all the answers
And I'm not perfect in anyway
But as a man I want to show you some pointers
that I learned along the way
In order to excell in your manifest
You have to know where to start
See 1st you have know God
And like be like David after his heart
This 1 step is critical
In determining if you succeed
Because how can you expect your family to follow you to God
If you don't know how to lead

A man doesn't define is life
With materialistic wealth
Yet he is secure in his weakness
And not afraid to ask for help

Yet a man doesn't owe a lot of debt
And pays back everything that he is lent
Because it's impossible to trust a man with money
Who won't even give God his 10 percent

He understands that things are earned
Nothing In life is given
A man will never settle
For a handout
He Will work to make
HIS living

A man doesn't give up on himself
When he feels life is too hard
And he'll gladly take care of his kids
Without looking for praise or an
award A man is a protector

THE FUTURE MIRACLE OF YESTERDAY

Always ready to defend
He is confident in who he is
So he doesn't have to pretend
A man has integrity and wisdom
Like a 3 piece suit he wears it well
In a society that's design for him to fall
He remembers he is the head and not the tail
A man is always hungry for knowledge
Doesn't settle for the status quo
He is humble and grateful for what he has
But is always willing to grow
A man takes responsibility
For the actions he choose
He won't imprison you with lies
But he will free you with the truth
A man has a sense of humor

Can make lemonade out of lemons
But the best way to identify a man
Is by the way he treats women
See he knows that the woman is his rib
Someone's daughter mother sister wife
And he understands not put his hands
On the species that gave him life
Ladies look at the men that surround you
Can they cultivate your life
If the answer no then be patient because it's
A man's blessing to find his wife

A man teaches his kid the bible
Like Ephesians 6:1-4
He does is so his childs name doesn't end up
Inmate 2y9684

So remember fathers

CEDRIC LOGAN

If you know the power you possess
And lives you have the ability to change
It is time we start stepping up as men
And not just making the claim

But they taking money out of schools
So they can home for us in jail
So a father job is to teach the future generations and lead
them out of hell
So I hope you have been blessed
With the nuggets that I have given
So now that have the tools
It is time we really live instead of just existing

FROM A KINGS POINT OF VIEW

When the pain still comes
Emotionally black and blue
How do you view the kingdom
From a Kings point of view

When you gave your very best
You just knew you gave your all
Trying to build up a queen
Who tried to cause the kingdom to fall

He gives the her the keys to the kingdom
A grave mistake on his part
Her venomous words is like a sword
Stabbing him in his heart

She fills his soul with despair
She refuses to be led
She kisses her king softly
After leaving a peasants bed

He raises the inherited princesses
He loved them as his own
The queen quietly plots with the children
To overthrow his throne

But alas

CEDRIC LOGAN

His exile was not his ending
But a journey he is forced alone
He had to leave behind his queen
Who only wanted his thrown

The king is publicly ridiculed
Taunted and put down
The royal family destroys his name
As the queen flaunts his crown

The kings heart is saddened
By the queens deceitful lies
He has to watch his old kingdom fall
With tears in his eyes

But like the spirit of the phoenix
The kings inner fire is rebirthed
He rebuilds a new a new empire
With the loving hands of Mother Earth

A miracle is born
The little child looks up the king
The true hier to the land
Knows her dad will do anything

So how does a man do it
A life's path how does one choose Well
How would you view your kingdom
From a Kings point of view

WARZONE

We living in the war zone where devils rivals
with us and we have to roll 20 deep like we riding the bus
But when you step in to the danger zone survival is a must
And if we do not stop killing each other there be no survival for us
Yea the word play is cool but you heard what I said right
Crooked cops protecting each other and those that got they bread
I mean you have fake neighbour watch people acting like they feds right
Killing kids in dead night and brothers getting killed for no taillights
Yea this world is crazy insane it needs a straight jacket
Sad thing is this evil never left it just went from mask to mask
But how you ask do we keep experiencing this blast from the past
Because you keep joy riding on the road to destruction thinking
    you'll never crash
The news always criminalizes the innocent slaughtered
Putting mugshot up to trying to justify the murder
My hands up don't shoot officer for real
I'm a father Im not doing anything illegal and I don't want to be
    harassed and bothered

No matter what state you living in right now we're in a state of War
You keep talking about Let Freedom Ring but you're scared to
    answer the call
You spend money to see 3 purge movies and still don't understand
    what you saw
That they using Walmart as a cover think about it the letters in
    name and you get martial law
Y'all better wake up and pay attention cause lifes schools is Session
Made it through Recessions and great depressions only to remain
    in oppression

Subjected to excessive force and wrongful uses of their weapons
Where they exclamation point that gun and shoot without ever
   being questioned
I can hear the critics now oh that's very black of me to speak out
   here and not be quiet to this nation's tragedy but as you sit
   back they break our back what more can you ask for me
   because I'm sick of this war and I'm tired of these casualties

THE ONE THAT NEVER WAS

Her hair was different colors
From the different wigs she had/
She had a mean body she flaunt her shades and Betsy Ross bag/
But she was so misguided super young when she lost her dad/
So she learned from sugar daddies how to get everything out a lad./
He didn't love himself but he tried to save the girl /
Heartbroken by hearing all the things that happened her world/
He took on her baggage he took on her scorn /
Searching for the companionship of a love that could be born //
Years ago and the remain together but yet are through//
They we destined for destruction from the moment they said I do//
between his social media and her multiple affairs//
Love became imprisoned bitterness resentment and betrayals//
Random acts of violence whether verbal or in fights//
He was concerned about his will bring but he feared for her life//
He lost who he was trying to be who she wanted him to be//
He tried to make to do the best he could but couldn't get her to see//
The sins of the past murdered the blessings of today
But the mysteries of tomorrow is a path they each have to pave

TIME

My time Our time
Live this time
Like it's the last time
The time is now
There is no time like the present
So please don't waste time
Because time is of the essence
Your timing has to be perfect
Because timing is everything
Time to live to live like kings
Time to love our Queens
The memories will be your timeline
And remember times will be rough
And that's the time to be strong until your time is up

THE INQUIRIES OF THE BROKE BUT NOT DEFEATED

Why do I remain restless melancholy through the night//
Trying to erase memories that have been branded in my mind//
Daydreams fantasies envisions of the perfect life//
Replaced by despair anguish broken heart and the pain in my eyes//
I gaze upon my life and wonder why am I even here//
A beautiful lie in public a smile to mask the tears//
To the world I am invincible my bravery blinds then from my fears//
My rampage illuminates the room filled with empty cheers//
I guess it remains mystery like the puzzle of time itself//
Trying to put it all together winding down into a deteriorating health//
But until you can endure the pain that you refuse to have felt//
How can rise from the ashes like a phoenix to help some body else

WAKE UP

Wake up why are you sleeping too the monster that we fear
So blind to the foreshadowed apocalypse that is finally here
warnings from regular people ignored while celebrity
speeches get cheered.
I guess you only real to you preach
Something they don't want to hear
We have to own our part to the mess that's been made
We see our brothers and sisters in the sun yet we sit in and throw shade
So quick to give an opinion to have something profound to say
Then say that is none of my business while sipping tea and lemonade
Wake Up
How many more of our people have die in despair
Trying to educate a generation that doesn't even care
Where they care less about what's in they had but the style of their hair
And kids that can whip and nae nae but don't know the Lord's prayer
Wake up
Time us winding down and there too much work to do
We need to be uniting not in cliques gangs and crews
A lot of things are uncertain but one thing you can prove
In order to make your dreams come true you here is a tip that you can use
Wake UP

I'M JUST SAYING

I look this generation and its not what I pictured
Seems like the future has become wicked wicked wicked wicked
Nowadays boys don't know their ABCs but so quick to prove they a G
And girl wanna exploit the body on social media to be an over-
    night celebrity
We living in a time of scandals that just doesn't seem to stop
Where society gossips about about the drama and not the love and
    the hip hop
Lemonade once a summer drink is now a national woman's album
Written about a man who said a chick wasn't one but he had 99
    problems.
Everybody talks about what they would do with everyone else is
    predicament
But then turn right back around sip tea and say it's none of my
    business
I'm just saying be the person in the mirror what do you have to lose
Your life your gold your destiny you have the power to choose
All hope of Humanity I want to see in you
So Just like the magic show Now You See Me 2